Cry of the Peacocks

Naomi Lazard

I saw how the night came,
Came striding like the color of the heavy hemlocks.
I felt afraid.
And I remembered the cry of the peacocks.
—WALLACE STEVENS, "Domination of Black"

Cry of the Peacocks

Harcourt, Brace & World, Inc., New York

First edition

Library of Congress Catalog Card Number: 67-10765

Printed in the United States of America

Some of the poems in this book previously appeared in *Chicago Choice, Chicago Review, Harper's Bazaar, Jewish Currents, Mainstream, Michigan Quarterly Review, Poetry Northwest,* and *The Virginia Quarterly Review.*

The quotation on the title page from "Domination of Black," by Wallace Stevens, is from *The Collected Poems of Wallace Stevens,* published by Alfred A. Knopf, Inc., and is used with their permission.

Contents

Elysian Jumps

 *Elegies*

Lot's Daughter

It was not us! The men with bullets
for eyes burned the malachite hills,
deflowered the jade, the emerald peaks,
and surrounded the rubbish with walls.
The enemy came in the eggshell darkness,
music deadened our sighs. I remember
the hall and the last concerto,
the tapestries hung between the pillars.
Battle scenes of Siena, farewells, horses
with their necks arching forward.
The marble arm of the saint stretched out
blessing and reblessing us. I was lost
in the beam of the music. I was bright as glass.

Then the blood, a living thing on the stairs,
purple and brown on the stone treads.
We ran as we were commanded, with our hearts
contracting like pulp and knocking
against our throats. Without looking back
I know the flare over the ruined hills,
a wild trace falls down my side and I continue
to run beating the ground with my heels
so as not to fall. I run like a hare,
like an animal wedged in a terrible trap
with spikes for sides. I run with my breath
leaving my lungs with the sound of sorrow.

It is all gone now, a spirit with no name,
And I. I never wanted to come this far.

Under the Rooms

The dry bushes exhale a dark shape
that turns and runs. . . .

My mother lying in a white room
with an extra bed
and snow erasing the windows.
I take her wax voice, her body
that has betrayed her, first the node,
the stranger living in her breast,
then the marathon, the thousand hours'
dance through black glittering spotlights
till her legs hang from her body.
I take her ruined thighs on my shoulders.

Her hair is still growing
through every chink, her breathing
exhausts me.

My mother dying, the animals
close to me between the sheets,
their claws in her hair, silently.
Their loving hurts me.

My mother is exhaled, a dark shape.
The dry bushes turning under my feet. . . .

The animals love each other forever.

Family Chronicle

GRANDMOTHER

More than once they said it:
She'll never do it, she'll never turn the knife
against herself. But the knife poised there
many times towards the anvil of her chest
and her screams raged through the halls
and shook the banisters while we slept
or were awakened by the knife clattering.

A momentary aberration, that's all it is.
She's so strong, the prow of the family.
She doesn't know her strength. Her emerald eye,
almost as real as the real one
keeps vigil in the kitchen.
The loaves of twisted bread stand high,
the candles shake their shadows on her.

The old house would sigh and list a little more
towards evening, the oilcloth slipped.
Friday nights, the ritual, the ceremonial foods,
the rubric passage into the Sabbath.
Years before in Kiev the venerable innkeeper,
her father, was pious and mused in his beard.
She slept over the stone stove there and dreamed
of ribbons. Sleigh bells interspersed
her garlands in the morning.

*

Four years in a sweatshop sewing blouses,
then marriage to Michael, also born in Kiev.
They did what they could in the Victorian twilight,
they opened a candy store and also sold cigars.
What could they do with their dreams but dream them
in the rooms over the store, in the night
that closes on the rooms like the backs of beetles.

A vast circling in the air:
the century beginning to the sounds of birth
and industry. The concert of the street
is furious with aspiration. It is different
from the ghetto. But the great-grandfather,
retired innkeeper and scholar of the Torah,
mutters the cabbala in his beard.
He is against Christmas and all pagan ceremonies.
An empty chair at the kitchen table
is waiting for the messiah.

From time to time she was uncertain.
Still young, she knew the danger was they would not learn
to salvage, that it would be difficult to change.
Michael is there to kneel beside her
and sing of previous hostels, yet these circles
drive a hard bargain. Once started
there is no reprieve.

In Philadelphia, in the rooms behind the candy store,
she became a matriarch, the link forged
between the old world and the new.
There never was time to be at bay,
she kept expanding. It was recorded in her stance,
her steady ramrod posture.

Evenings around the great shining table
held promises of future explorations. The son
would be a mathematician, the daughters would be
educated too. Ruth had the solitary gift of music
and practiced her violin. Rosalyn had a ruffled dress
that swept around her when she graduated normal school.

Poverty is always present, or very nearly.
But thanksgiving as well for escape from pogroms.
Thank God for the candy store, for the regular customers,
for the back yard, for the Succoth house
and all its blessings. They hang from the ceiling—
bunches of grapes and baskets of apples, walnuts too.

Or later in the snow-bandaged streets, waiting
all night and the next day for Caruso:
those were the days when singing became everyone
and arias from Verdi trebled out of the victrola.
Michael and Ben stood their ground
outside the Academy of Music, Anna lit the beaded lamps
and joined them in her best shirtwaist
and trailing skirt, her costume completed
by a tender brooch and gloves with intricate buttons.

Like years the years sweep past
leaving in their wake a more pronounced posture,
an everlasting determination. Clean,
it must be clean enough to eat on the floor.
The sour cream and cucumbers must be fresh
each afternoon. The books must be read,
the accounts paid, the cigars and candy renewed.
She is dauntless and energetic, always there
for everyone, Anna who is brave and cheerful,

who is firm as a backbone, who is the heart of the house.
Michael tends the store; it's a job he can do
without compromising his simplicity,
without leaving Puccini and Gounod.

Once walking, she finds a leaf has fallen
and it is nostalgia that dismembers
the accounts due, the stock of cigars
and piled-up books and papers. Back there,
before these accidental properties they never really chose,
was a sort of beauty and time for contemplation.

What's the use of industry, esprit de corps?
My life has a real home somewhere
outside these systems and certainties.
The ghost of an evening heaves itself
upon a frosty afternoon, on the snow-mullioned windows,
and suddenly I'm in another country,
more familiar. I hear horses and sleighs sliding.
Here it's a trolley car racketing down the street
with its horseshoe fender. Or meanwhile,
inside an upstairs room my mirror speaks
the curious dreams that nibble away at time.
The portent of these wrinkles near my eyes
I cannot read, nor qualify the future
more than I have done.

Still alive he looked like death
had overtaken him. Anna scolded his pallor
and wrapped him in comfort on the mohair sofa.
Ah, who will be with him, who
will hold a candle for him?
He could hardly move but he would go

outside to buy a china doll or two
for the grandchildren. Michael's passion
is tender as his life, and almost mute.
It roared only in music.
Now he is little more than a twig,
broken and slight on his sofa.
He needs almost no space at all.

He lived to see his son a mathematician,
his daughters married, and two grandchildren
sliding down the banisters. He lived to see
the depression scuttle the store.
He saw the old innkeeper weep in his beard.

When he died he was missed bitterly
as sweetness, or love that said a late
and last goodbye. Where is his music?
Who can trace his long footprint in the passage?
"Where is Michael?" the neighbor children ask.
Where is the candy man, the joke paper man,
the music listener, the singer?
The candy store troubadour has passed away from our street.

She harbored his dying skull like a great white jewel
and faced it nightly. She brushed her rough red hair,
took out all the pins, changed the linen
and crocheted heavy tablecloths in ivory and white.
She patterned the house with her handiwork.
Her emerald eye (the false one) stared emptily
at old account sheets, all paid, paper
paving stones for a family. She is excellent
with longing, a severe indomitable woman.

MOTHER

She sits in a photograph framed in bouffant hair,
one hand trailing over a fern;
behind her a birdcage hangs. The date: 1910.
The future: sweet if you fall in with the eyes
and the feeling in them. The facts: otherwise.
Because she is handsome and her face graven
with certain qualifications, at once
delicate and bold. Her black hair like sculptured
shadows. She has a serious name
and legitimate talent.

Anna is the focus of energy around the kitchen table
and a stern mentor. To call this woman mother,
to be loyal to her wisdom, means relinquishing much.
        (There is no accident more comprehensive
        than the one of birth; from that moment
        we are compounded. Certain doors are open,
        certain distances seem available. Largely,
        most are unsuspected or remain like images
        of a beloved place, dimly seen or felt as if our lives
        fathom a breadth there, but have lost that country.
        Yet it can come suddenly, a flicker of desire
        for the other side of closed doors;
        or it may quicken in unsuspected streets.
        While all the time like a dinosaur
        with a very small head, and ponderously turning
        toward one thing or another, we move,
        but before we arrive it is already gone.)
Is it that one never knows until very late,
maybe too late, just what has been abandoned?

And then, wherever we find ourselves to be,
in a hotel bedroom with a wet dawn diffusing light
to grey, or a four-flight converted brownstone,
it seems too late to reconsider. Too late to start again.

In a photograph she sits in a dress of dark stuff
and white stockings. Somewhere behind her tilted head
a half seen birdcage hangs. The house is full
of ferns and rubber plants that spread a green
gentility. Spring has struck a different note
this year; the trumpet tulips sway and gallantly
surrender their crimson plan to us. Rebecca
possesses only her emotions and they are rough;
she talks an edge between ambition and desire.
She can't escape the relentless expectations
of family and turns her forces toward a concert,
practices her violin daily. When the night arrives
she finds her fear of falling short too difficult.
The recital continued without her.

After that debacle she played only for herself
and to the cane backs of chairs.
Her violin became a catafalque
holding the bones of her aspirations.

In the unalterable climate of family
she is misunderstood, but the starting places
are graciously set forward. They say
that being beautiful is a career, or at least
an occupation signifying something important.
They say never mind, you are a woman;
don't be too hard on yourself. You are a woman

whose black eyes are too magnificent to hold.
Off stage or on you are still lovely. Take care,
oh take care; marry a sure man, a man on his way upward.
So she married an embroiderer, a designer of flowers.

Nobody we care for is actually a liar
but wheels once started continue to spin.
The perpetual motion of the mind
is like a hand out in the weather.
The last line of his letters reads love,
but what is wrong is larger than promises.
Still, in spite of this it is the hour
in her eyes for pleasure. The city is graceful
in November; there is a delicate promise of frost
as two figures leave the factory. Nothing seems lost.
If it's belief she wants, this man at her side
deserves it. Altogether, it's good.
They know privation and that's a bond too;
meanwhile there is delight.

Where are those beginnings
that determine our end? Is it a candy store
shuttered and dark as a boudoir,
uneven stacks of magazines and jars of colors
shifting in an ancient light? Is it the mother
who is an engine, whose mechanism
casts the dimension of longing? Is it the father,
mild as milk, certain only that suffering
is bearable mixed with humor, or at a concert?
Is it all of these and more?
Is it also the dark realm of memory
of something we have never known

but have imagined after many tellings,
like the two-month journey over water
and the ship rolling, like the festival of arrival
turned bitter and uncomprehending?

They lived in the old house too
in an upstairs bedroom facing the yard.
The gentle color of the morning quickened
on the casement, threw salmon-freckled fish
across the cover, passed coins over their shoulders,
and they were rosy with the morning.
It seemed early everywhere.
If a door slams somewhere it is the wind foreclosing.
Here it is unpretentious, but quick with zeal.
Forces they don't control are cavalier;
unlike them, energies beyond their control
betray their labor and grind down their desire.
It is so easy to find only oneself wanting
especially after many attempts, especially
after failure. And so difficult to put one's finger
on just what went wrong; sometimes it seems
she is an idiot in reverse—confounded by simplicity.

I don't want to scrutinize that black cloud of hair
or say exactly when I noticed the factory in her heart.
Yes, I have a machine in my heart
that manufactures bitter apples for my table
and nails for my soup. Though the tablecloth
is clean and white, the candles lit,
there is always a dead grape in the center.
And a curtain blowing, hesitating
on the threshold of desire.

✿

Her growing older meant my own fall forward.
To the same regrets? The heart of the factory
is an apple corer, turning
and spitting out the same seeds.
>*Who can tell the core from me?*
>*If wit and bitterness are the same things*
>*I am cursed with a double sword. And ultimately*
>*I dare to use them both as final weapons*
>*against myself as well.*

It was envy hung over her like never worn garments
on the line of her aspiration.

The candles weep; Rebecca and Maurice
play duets in the front room over the store
when he is home. In the amber afternoon
some petals fall, sprinkling the table and the floor
as if a hand had thrown largesse there.
They took what was theirs once
like those swans that sail the lily pond,
but you might say they chanced everything
on Friday when all the time the calendar read Saturday
in black and white. Now she is more careful.
That summer is gone under the ground.

In a photograph she faces the sea,
one hand holding a stone. Like a bronzed carving
roughened by weather too, she has long
acquaintance with the storms of forsaken
enterprise. This has left her weak
but her laugh shakes easily,
her arms are round and dark.
>*Where are those circles which enclose comfort,*
>*where the sting of love's long rapier is blunted?*

Everything is acquired at last,
even the talent to relinquish what we know.

I know that the roads as I travelled them
fell gasping away like bees buzzing behind,
with fragrance of honey falling, falling,
into a sea far below.
And when the sun has been scattered
over the city; when I rejoiced in the burnished
spaces between leaf and leaf; when I was young
as a bird is young and wore ropes of clover
braided on the slopes of my celebration—
When I stepped out to the ribboned distance
where the low fog lies like a dusky dish
served up for breakfast—
The key to my house is lost among the clover,
living always a little beyond me, receding
under the fog, glancing on lakes of tin.

The obituary will hardly say it:

Rebecca Carlitz, December 13, 1955;
to be autopsied for pathology
then cremated—that her blue ashes
may regenerate the earth;
that her crisp eyebrows may burn their way upward
(in life they seemed like wings)
and she, like a sleeper in May
who will never awaken to summer anywhere.

FATHER

He left her to go to sea, the embroiderer,
the self-made mariner, and would return
from time to time like a god from the water,
something subterranean lighting his narrow eyes.
He would come straight from the ship
tasting of salt and adventure.

There was a bower, a kind of arched foyer
leading to a storeroom behind the candy store.
My father stood there in his shirt sleeves
with darkness behind him and darkness ahead.
He stood in his white shirt sleeves
wearing a small moustache and a narrow look
and his knowledge of the sea.
Petty officer of a small craft, guardian
of the best, the unresigned, the anti-bitter.
Master of beauty who taught me everything
he knew, maestro who noticed countries
in clouds, eyes the color of dead leaves,
goblets crystalled in the falling snow,
a wand suddenly appearing in the rainbow.
Yes. That's the man, poised now for a minute
in that bower in his shirt sleeves
with his collar open and the column of his throat
suggesting action and a grace only bestowed
by love or some other major accomplishment.

A pebble in my shoes between my toes,
the sun drips fire on the stones.
A stretch of broken road and then the beach,
a sleep of gulls, an interval of laughter.

There was a cottage in Wildwood
with summer shining like light
flashing from a blade, stinging and sweet
as a bite from a eucalyptus leaf.

I hear that laughter even now.
Yet he might be dead too; suddenly
one morning splashed with flowers
it might be nothing mattered to him
any longer but his next breath or the next
beat of his heart. I have listened
for his step and have heard the night hooting.
I remember the songs:
Why is a round table? And why
is a red ball? Why is a crooked letter?

There was too much quicksilver;
paint was made of it and music. Waking
he dreamed leaves turning curiously
over his wrist, leaving a mark there.
And spoke these leaves turning, they crumble
out of his mouth leaving colors there.
It might be he could have been simple
with a harpsichord or a lute
in a Botticelli setting, or easy
if all the gardens belonged to everyone.
The mote in his eye was the easy winning,
the next chance for everything.
He would disappoint you: his promises
were like jewels he couldn't afford.
It was like that with the dolls' house,
steeplechase, the visit to Coney Island.
The memory of these promises never kept

became nostalgia for future assignations.
There were vine leaves twisted in his hair
but the hero had died, had lost
his inner resonance. He wore yellow spats
and carried a cane. Oh, a man
to be afraid of, an unsound man,
a jack of all trades, a permanent discontent,
a nonchalant dapper man on a flying trapeze.

But in 1938 he had no winter coat
and wore a grey pencil-striped suit.
Highly polished shoes. No hat. No gloves.
He leaned into the future, only lacking
a winter coat to keep him warm.
That was before he went to jail for fraud,
before he struck it rich there
with his friends, the tax evaders.
They formed a club up there in Lewisberg.
That was three rooms in Brooklyn
and the sea behind him, that was when
his name was Devereaux and was the boss
of a bowling alley. It was before he went bald
except for a small fringe, and before
the tinted spectacles, delicate and rimless,
before the diamond ring on his pinky, before,
oh long before, the rows of suits and coats
hung in his closet. It was before
any of us imagined such great things.

Then look! We haven't been poor for nothing,
we've produced a winner, a capitalist!
There was a war on and it was good for business.
We needed shoes and hats, gloves and silk dresses,

charge accounts and trips to the theatre,
lingerie, a Magnavox, a baby grand,
flowers for D-day, for V-day. I was a growing
American child with plans for a higher education
and a tangible future.
Then it all came down with a thud.
You see, Madam, it's really simple.
We expect such behavior from a man like this.
A borderline case, yes, we might say psychopathic.
A character disorder, a disturbed balance,
a listing moral sense, the judgment goes under.
It is a tragedy, he was a misfit,
a loser, a bad one, a loose screw, a ruin.

And I was splashed with his colors
but the actual man is gone.

He went that-a-way, there, through that alley.
He is playing chess at the club downtown.
Or was he last seen driving a convertible
towards New York City?
                              Why not Central America
strumming a guitar and holding a cup?
A quixotic figure with his bald head
and tinted spectacles.
                              Did he tell you to meet him
in LA? Never mind. By now he's on board
a fast ship and heading for Le Havre, all points east.
A curious stocky man, a heavy-lidded
paunchy (oh, only just) man? Yes.
Seen in Rio, Caracas, Lima, Guadalajara.
That's the man! Cooking for the sailors,
strumming his guitar. Of course.

And smiling usually, very friendly
to birds and dogs, packing an artist's case.
Want to know more? Call the consulate,
the local precinct, the provost, the bailiff,
or the night watchman at any chess club.

He is tuning in on the ocean with his pitchfork
and following the notes well.
He is napping . . . the sleep of innocence,
dreaming of the days he was a big spender,
lying on the wind and snoozing
happily . . . an infinity of bees.

CONFLAGRATION FOR MY SISTER

We sat in identical housecoats
                                faces scrubbed
clean as porcelain or fresh-picked berries
after our bath
Our home was a burning building
                                it touched
a plentiful garden too that burned
we sat where they placed us
                                and copied their denials
which burned our eyes and fingertips

Our mother of despair who waited in the kitchen
Our father of futility who broke jail but never left it
They showed us
                the way up is always more heavily guarded
                than the entrance

❉

It wasn't the same rope we held for the exit
rather, we tumbled out like a couple of sad clowns
in the opening number of the circus

You found the way between steel and paper
the way out across injections and bandaged arms
waiting to be amputated
                          and hearts blooming on operating
                                                      tables
Looking out of the window
                          you see thirty thousand
                          doomed cases
                          waiting for admission
it is the obituaries that never lie

You sit at the window
                          still somewhat intact
                          watching the fog spin down

                          you walk the grey embankment
                          in your strong box of a city

(In Trafalgar Square the admiral sits—or stands
high enough to tell the time by Big Ben's hands
below his feet the pigeons coo and cry)

You wind a ball of orange wool
                          above goldfish and minnows
                          and canaries with gold teeth
                          and underwear hanging on a
                                                      line

*

You wind a ball of green wool
                above black horses with manes like clouds
                and empty suitcases left in furnished rooms
                with wallpaper designed by the blind

You walk down the embankment
                surrounded by lost cab drivers
                with silvery necks and frost bitten ears
                pursued by bicycles with no drivers

You arrive at the laboratory
                above cellars where geraniums
                are incurable wounds
                and wheelchairs idle beside the desks

In the afternoon
                the grey street closes and sleeps
                you are tired too
                it's a long way you have run
                in your little knit dress

                All down the length of the street
                the houses are burning!

they are burning with the same color as your hearts
as they lie exposed and dying on the operating tables.

Often This Winter

Often this winter, drinking coffee in the morning,
looking out at skeletons of trees
whose flesh of leaves is dead, I assemble
another vista. Do you remember,
out of the reaches of all our mornings,
an almost unnoticeable one, conventional
as a cloud, grey and rainy,
which might easily be lost in time?
We had a window curtained in cotton
through which light passed fitfully across our bed.
"A typical morning," we said, "and it won't get better."
We rose, drank orange juice and coffee
and ate bread and butter. It was a failure
of a morning, failing to kindle desire,
failing to satisfy. We were cold in that house,
there was a war. You rustled the *Tribune* unhappily.
But now I remember your skin was amber
and you photographed me in the bright cold garden
under that same window, under those fleshless trees.

A curious morning to recall now this victorious winter.

For You, Sidney

For you
>   God created too many gargoyles
>   who knock against each other in a night of stone:

>   the noise
is like the rumor running the halls of an asylum
that the guards have all been overpowered
and their arms pinned back like absurdities,
their lolling heads
>   torn from any purpose.

The latest communiqué concerns this night
that vapors on the window with a bitter rain
assembling images that melt and separate;
the slow motion of a dying brain.

The gravel of voices is close at hand
and the smell of an elevator
where bodies fuse together
in a rough encounter:

>   we hooked
like safety pins on a torn blouse or a brassiere strap
and in the melee we stumbled
over our battered seasons
and gave each other terrible names

*

In the confusion I turned.
                              I found you magnified
shorn, a giant captive speck in the lens of my telescope.
I saw you strutting in your stone disguise
arm in arm with the ambassador of stone.
His hateful archduke Pap kissed you on the nose.

Later your caress
was a brick wall falling on me.
We slept in iron positions
                              twisted on handlebars
borne on that bicycle
to an earlier prevented wish.

If the Victims Would Testify

What was regretted here, what voices mingled
with the sighs of tapestries
moving on the heavy air?
And when the china smiles were handed round
whose knee was pressed accidentally?
After all, what else could we have said, what else?
It is too late, too much has happened.
Look at the results. There is a woman
remembering her dead mother in the middle of lunch.
Such memories are unnerving
surrounded by Russian sable. But I listened.

Tell me, what else could we have done
alone in a dangerous city when all the lamps were lit?
The old guard sweeping along the tracks
said he hadn't been home for forty years.
His marbled eyes looked out like accidents.
I had the certainty that everything could end like this.

The first time was easiest, quick snap of calling cards
printed in four languages assured my hand.
I waited on the landing long enough
to see the others leave. I stood until it was too late,
of course, again. I watched you in the photographs,
younger, dark hair against a dark brocaded chair,
saw you where the honeysuckle sang
and where the oleander, red and white,
infused the afternoon.

As I removed my gloves, I said,
"I promise you I can be convenient as a travelling iron
and fold up small enough to feel like home"—
and leaned on the balustrade and almost fell.

How could you know how late it was for me?
Or how rich I am in promises.
You couldn't hear my other voice, the silent one breaking,
"Then if no survivors leave but only masks
that tell their own story, why do you whisper?
Here in the park with the beech trees and the stony grass
it is too late to start again."

Could it be possible after such confession
to be graceful for you in the garden
or quietly read a book and wait?
There is the photograph of course; I took it
and held it a long time before it dropped
like some bright feather out of the train window.

October 8–11, 1963: Rome

In that season the days were shorter leaving in their passage an unbearable feeling of loss and promises. All week long I had been waking up, trying to assemble something usable from the rag ends of the past year. We were walking, I remember, across some freshly thrown gravel, the grounds of an itinerant carnival. It was still warm. I saw you were wearing crepe-soled shoes that bounced a little each time you stepped forward.

"I've thought of you all this time . . . everywhere."

"You've thought of me and I am always here just the same.
It is all the same as it always was. This is life, this
moment. You think of me and yet you forget how it happens."

"No. I do not forget it ever."

"All the same you have never submitted. You store up your life
as if it were grain, as if it will last, as if some time
in the future you will be able to open the doors and take it out
intact, each kernel full of treasure."

"How strange you know these secret arrangements."

"And what will you have finally? I tell you this is the moment,
it is upon us. It has been patient all these years."

We walked to the river. There were no sounds in the night except your breath.

❋

"It is like infancy to stand here looking out
but what a strange infancy! Corrupted already.
And the other bank is too yellow or russet
for remembering; there is not enough light
on the water. It is all there in the windows.
Rome is a peculiar fever, promising
slow, occasional recovery after the crisis.

You are yourself a crisis, don't you know it?
Would you believe your memories are legible
as ramparts on your face? I mean the ones
confusing cold with hunger, I mean the ones
that bind me. They are like this city,
constant, dangerous, wounding as all real beauty.
Quick then, what am I to do? You—with your gestures
like propitiations to some restless god.
You don't know what divides us. . . ."

"Your life is like an old costume locked in an attic
you haven't had time to try. It is an old game,
solitary, useless. For this you won't forgive me."

"No. You've said it."

"In my own language . . . perhaps."

"In your own language . . . like light on the water."

Contrary to my purpose (if I had a purpose) we did go to
Tivoli. Just as he said it is a summer palace, not meant for
wind, not meant for loneliness. We swept like leaves across
high passes and dropped finally behind the failing crowds and
unfamiliar rooms. Then it was too late for denials; we sailed

on down waters of the night in our little craft, our boat of reeds and whispers until the morning.

"It will be cold too soon. Already I feel bandaged by this wind. Our faces that had opened are contained."

Song at the End of Summer

Look, it's still hot on the horizon,
the sun is naked orange swallowing the light.
Soon when the bulbs string out
along the dunes, when the sea sticks
on round heelmarks in the path
what will we have lost?
The words are gone as our attempts
to say them, gone like those seven swallows
we saw once posed for a minute on the swingpost.

I always thought tenderness dangerous,
the sea wind stroking the path an unavoidable
nostalgia. What ugliness, I said at first,
and planned to make this house auspicious.
Nobody will know how I have failed
though the lawn was faithfully watered.

That which I leave behind, like you,
like these cuttings of Bougainvillaea dying,
dripping their color on the clear glass,
can be easier now. Nothing more is expected.
No one I know walks here any more, only a grey cat
curious about the new tenants
and to watch moths fling themselves
against the windows.

I hadn't the sure foot either for the crevice
broken between our differences.
I hadn't the great heart.

Party on Lake Shore Drive

The words I've said before,
the gestures are the same.
There's not enough moonlight in the room
to whitewash them. About our heads
the nimbus of success balloons.
I count upon my face to speak for me.
In 20th-century attitudes
we take each other like a drug,
the glass reflects our arabesque
repeating the worn-out rogueries.
All the beautiful things that fly are quiet.

We are illicit here; it's not the first time.
Yet I would rather step upon the border
of the light and sink into the air
than continue to exchange these perfidies.
I settle for politeness.
Suddenly, Amanda cries, grieving
for some offense committed to her childhood
dignity. She looks at me as if I were not the one
who buried mine still wet and long ago
in dark lagoons where black birds fly
and the green silt loosens dangerously.

Later in the dark, alone,
watching the frozen spaces of the night,
I think of Amanda. Must children
always do my weeping for me?

 *Arrivals*

The Bird

It was necessary to turn back
through the clouds hanging over the mountains,
up the road that curved and climbed higher
than birds' nests, higher than their flight.
We heard a thump like a small stone falling
but I had seen the bird coming out of the cloud
swerving to avoid a collision. Giosi said,
"But it's dead. It must be dead already."
I saw him there hidden and panting
behind the license plate. "No, he's not dead,
only stunned and frightened. Give him a minute
to recover." And Giosi was ashamed. "It's so easy
to hide hope, so easy to accept the dead bird,
the unalterable wounds already inflicted,
all abstractions, and pass on."
But face to face with the living bird,
feathers startled out of place, foot crooked
chillingly, beak opening and closing without a sound
we feel his terror and his fragile life.
Face to face with his warm body, his brown eye
searching, his head askance in an agony of strain,
we stood quietly heavy with tenderness.
And the bird took his chance, wanting only
a few moments for the chill to leave him,
gathered his will and flew off
into the steep Tuscan twilight, circling
once around the bend of our love, then straight out
and up the feathery line of our hope
to where they all live, invisible, in the cloud.

Lines for My Birthday

It is a spiked March day,
the palings of the wind fence
sharpened to perfection.
My friends support me
saying there is still time
for discoveries, but the morning
leans heavily. There are clocks
in the windows of every store
and watches that advise the year.
It seems the buried deaths I've died,
the lost seas of love, have overtaken me.
(Eurydice, running past the dark
planes of glass that grey her image
stops at a corner and waits for a bus,
tattoos her footsteps on the concrete curb.)
The secret deaths are never hidden well enough!
Oh, if only they could be rings
to wear around my fingers
or like my dresses hanging silent
in the closet. But I know it is very late.
My moving eye notates remainders.
But everyone is here on the corner
waiting for a bus, hopping like sparrows
on the bare uncovered ground.
It is the rain I miss.

Metropolitan Night

The night, wearing a dark hat, flashing
its smile, tapping its patent-leather toes.
The building across the street
where they dance on the second floor,
their shadows moving quickly as mice
against the windows.
                  The night tilts its hat
further down, lifts a corner of its smile
in that George Raft way. Somewhere in the park
someone is waiting for someone.
A darker shadow than the trees.

I've turned out my drawers looking,
shifted pile after pile of papers
for that one scrap that eludes me.
The document, the photograph, the license,
the writ. The drawing done quickly on a napkin.

The stirring is the same, everyone
is sleeping in the same positions, breathing.
The noises climb through the walls
and the night takes them in its gloved hands.
Now it's turning, turning
in a terrible pavane of stillness.

Someone has found someone in the park.
Shadows more silent than the trees.
My knuckles are white from too much listening
against the windows.

The Deceivers

To whom have you spoken today
of the dreams, the white-hot bands of pain
across your chest and back, of the usual sacrifices,
of the factories preparing our death?
Who did you meet out of the crowd and summon
with a little wave of your hand or a smile?
Why did you, leaning over the river,
almost fall into it, dreaming of the letter in your pocket?

With what aplomb did you dissemble
to your dearest friends thinking,
"They'll never know how much I'm really in the dark."
Under what pretenses did you order a pair of shoes
or a hat, while all the time
you knew this to be a temporary measure.
And didn't you sit under an electric eye and eat
while your appetite was forgotten
in the contemplation of midnight hair,
black or blond, and alive?

Ah with what assurance you did dissemble
until it seemed your voice was really right
and the stroke of the salesman's hand on your leg
turned its marble into flesh.
Your assurance astounded me. I believed it.
I castigated my own distress
and hurried into a café
to read the latest speeches of the senators
saying how the vote must be a victory for order. . . .

I looked up from my paper to see your face
saying yes, I am alive, and I believed it to be true.

A week will pass this way, and another.
I will wonder who is entering through the revolving door,
ordering a brandy and opening his paper
and flicking the thought of your midnight hair
in and out of the speeches.

Our Journey

The windows of the night.
Your slow white legs.
The ocean should be close, the white beach
where an animal separates itself from the sand
at the water's edge
and begins to move relentlessly
toward the dunes
as if it were figuring out its life.
The beach expands forever.
With the same motion your hand is figuring out my life.

The endless sand
leads to one strip of light
flickering among the curtains
like the half-closed eyes of that animal.

We are here
already halfway covered with sand.

After a Painting by Marc Chagall

Lying in the leaves are only two
deep in the close air
thick with the scent of those bright enduring flowers,
resting in the budding twigs
down in the private thickets,
side by side, and still.
Sharing the secret cave in the heart of secrets.

There is languor here. There is something
like a cadence dropping from the petals,
a kind of final circumstance
that has nothing to do with time or effort.
It happened yesterday or will happen tomorrow,
secretly, like the heart of a flower opening.

October Evening

I said the moon was rolling
toward the midnight, and drunkenly,
audaciously, attends a feast,
is merry at table though she is a spinster.
And I have a bunch of yellow flowers
in an orange bowl, a small rapport
with that one, and I have relinquished
all the days, the evenings, and mourn nothing.
Oh maybe a little trace of sun and fever,
maybe regret sleeps beside me sometimes
like a sister. If the stars are maudlin
I can blame the season, the colors
in the woods are too high for beauty.
I haven't said the worst is over.
The barbs loose in the air haven't lost
their sweetness. There is no letter
brought by the mailman can cajole me.

But moons are moons, there are millions
of them. And the birds fly
in ever widening circles.

The Dinosaur in the Museum

In this room are bones that hang together,
strung immobile in an attitude,
a certain stance that delicate and bold
(pause between a complicated entrechat
and pirouette), formed to the stern baton
of those old dancing masters,
time and exigence. Here
in the anteroom of history
the silences of centuries curl in shadows.
The giant neck and sloping tail
that drop like a parabola describe the skeleton.
All alone, the opalescent bones
string out their elegy. A hole
that lodged a slow eye in a slower needle head
returns my scrutiny. An odyssey of death
has ruined him. In the next room
our potsherds pile their messages.
It is cold in this museum.
I slide like a whisper, find my way
through corridors that wind to an enormous door.
A final push and the sun will open my face,
the skeins of my own life's web
pull me along.

Dress Her in My Shadows

Lift her through the leaves of a summer day.
Open the window, let the sun pour over her
and spill from her lashes.
Fill the bowls with jonquils, find an instrument
to dangle from the wind;
it should have the shape of a Chinese horn,
it should make a sound like water.
Clear out the closets, bandage all the mirrors
so they won't betray our secrets.

Dress her in my shadows, there is no danger.
I am further away than you imagine.
It is hot here too with an intense raging light,
the light needed by mariners and surf riders
and all those who live on precipices and defy falling.

Give her the gift of my places, all my desires.
Tear up the paper of our days and make confetti for her.
Sprinkle her with confetti until she is festive,
turn her on the wheel until you feel my edges.
While the moonlight melts to make her winning
untangle me from your branches.
Give her our darkness where recognition fails.

I am further away than you want to know,
here where the passage turns mightily
into another night, where terrible birds
unfold their wings. I am here,
far away, on the perilous side of the water.

A Letter to a Few Old Friends

I know this afternoon.
I know this obdurate silence, this flowering,
This rain of black petals.
It is there in the water glass, there
Unabashed, visible between the leaves.
It is my head loose on the pillow next to me
That turns and questions everything I've settled.
It is the letter I must write soon
To our old friends—and I still sit shuffling cards,
Crisping their edges as I would crumble bread.

The leaves of cards fall delicately into my hands
Face down—and I am safe from the one-eyed queen,
The grimacer, the one whose diamond floats
Beyond her reach though she strains her one
Bright eye across her cowl, though she turns
Her shoulder almost enough.

I want to say my life isn't a lie any more.
Gus, I have to tell you something about this day;
I wish I could go back a thousand thousand hours
or take your hand. . . .
I want Eve to know my poverty;
                              for I have walked
                              like those Spanish ladies
Who were never seen without their monkeys.
And Bill, remembering me, will agree.
Sonja, something should be won out of this failure.
Something should happen, some rapprochement.

But in the end I have resisted nothing:
                              I am the one-eyed queen
Whose solitary diamond is a monkey
That dances to many names on bent knees.

Naked after my bath I pull the shade
And pour out the water.
I wish I could pour myself out like water.
Instead I am fast in the form of a woman;
The cards slip from my hands one by one.

I've turned her up, the one-eyed queen
Whose famous diamond is melted in the water,
Whose monkey withered in the dance,
And she and I alone will write our letter.

Study for a Travel Book

It is six o'clock and a table has been ordered
to celebrate the evening. The day has passed quickly
as any ritual, for we have barely time enough to meet
or remark the beauty of the weather
before the shops are closed. A fitful light
illuminates the moment. For this brief time
I see you as you are, and have to leave.

In the pointed shadow of the obelisk
three American ladies sit
and mark the hours as they drop from time.

There is the darkness opening and shutting;
eighteen years with one man, and how they never
managed to escape, how it rains at least once every day.
They drink, exchanging similarities.
Apart from this adventure
there is a song troubling the colonnade
promising to those who want to give, another choice.

Further across the rain in a baroque hotel
the divorcee from California in her amethyst ensemble
and fresh-mown hair
sits elegantly like a piece of crystal about to break;
waits for her new young man while the back of every head
resembles her lover of three years ago.
. . . Wasn't it you I noticed there beside the railing
leaning over the empty air?
I was expecting you to come and save me. . . .

She wrote him five letters before she left
explaining exactly where and when she would be
in Roma, Milano, Firenze, Assisi.
We walk like mirages through real streets
leaving the click of heels on marble.
We are paper folded figures
opening with all our arms.

Who doesn't know the cats by moonlight
on the stones surrounding the Pantheon?
Or the door in the second column
that leads to a frieze of pensiones, amber hued
and shaded by lush plane trees all in bloom,
where only Italian is spoken
and the police never come.
For if the moment were now, and the afternoon
soft around the colosseum; if politeness or ease
were answers, who wouldn't choose to be there?
Behind the slatted windows a lacy gloom
settles on the couch and a wide awakening
shivers inside some well-loved eyes.

Hands that are young but seem compassionate
lie beside my own on the wet stone.
It is easy to forget who I am.
I touch the fabric of your coat to feel you near,
only have time for such important things
as noticing the way the shadow of your lashes falls on me.
The only thing forbidden is the thought of another summer;
even a long look out of the window will speak
too urgently of distances. We stop here
and live as if we have a thousand years.

Even when we're sure of our stop
(on number 98, at the abrupt turn from Gregorio VII)
I am often afraid to descend.
I remember I am a stranger;
unknown summers are hidden inside my pillow.
After serious study the bright red scar on your cheek
where the war struck you engages my interest
to the point of distraction.

I forbid myself persimmons, sometimes all red fruit.
We are like two figures in a grove
because here it is enough to be still
while the sounds from the arcade mingle
with the wind on the shutters like the chatter of teeth—
and let our lives fall where they will.

A Stop Near the Beach

"It remains to rediscover our life
now that we have nothing left any more."
—*George Seferis*

And stopping I turned to cast my glance
over the field which had rusted
A golden hare (I swear it was golden)
rushed to escape. So this is the way
creatures hide their lives
                              in the tall brown grass
with a frenzy of astonishment and a leap.
I've never outdistanced my eyes.
How many midnights have they awakened
like the eyes of statues left insecurely sealed?
It is the same now.
This rush of marble is the wind
rolling the stones in, smoothing indentations.
It is all the same as yesterday.

Here is where a child dropped a half-eaten peach
with the flower inside, dormant.
Thinking about what lies unrevealed
in the center of that stone
I carefully avoid it.
                              It is inedible,
no longer beautiful, an object to be noticed.
These fragments, noticeable in their own right,
still leave everything to be desired.
Nothing has been granted by the startled hare
or the remains of the peach,
                              only another moment.

*

Now that nothing is left there is only time.
There are these woods, this small clump
of summer flowers, this insistent murmur.
The reprise of the wind.

One White Cat

My wishes burn with the sound of a wounded cat
who knows the heavy thud or frank of nights,
and steals her sustenance among the porticos;
as my heroes have stolen my wishes away from me.

But they left me the small sad faces
who beg forgiveness for being so.
They left me Neptune spitting water like a God should,
and the speckled cats in the Pantheon.
(Ah, my dainty cats are washing after their meal
of bones and scraps; let us think together
how to escape the menace of the blind man's stick.)
They left me ruins of Palatine; the golden house
of Livia; a garden of stones.
And honey bread each morning baked before
I am awake, and the crescent butternuts.
They left me a final meeting in the crypt
where we watch the ghosts who silently among us
turn their repentance out like dust.
They left me velvet flowers in the straw,
tissue crumbled in the finery; the dance is dead.
Only the fountains are dancing in the square
with the cats on the cobbles, whiskers wild.
They left me my confession signed when you abandoned me,
and the sweet fat shoemaker's boy
who knows I only understand "Good evening";
whose dimples have an aptitude for joy.
They left me a hood and a domino
and a ticket to the masquerade of Fools;

and they left me a good hand, not the one on fire.
(I've handled too many roses, and I'm glad.)

So we will not grieve for those who ruined us,
but clasp our hands around a table, send out bread
and sweeter gifts; keep our fancies for the masquerade.
You see me now; don't say you have no clock
that strikes the same hour all night long.
Only empty the room of veils and we can meet
each other finally, and fold our ease instead.

For the year is getting old among the olive trees,
and we pay for our summer many times.
At the first frost in the carnival of thieves
through the whirling dance of masks.
To the whisper of shutters as they close,
and in the magnolia thickets.
At the end of the courtyard to the persistent slap
of golden sandals brilliant in the passage.

Still all my treasures walk beside me
saying the things I've heard of; change, begin.
Then everything within me moves toward you.
Thousands of fountains ringing round the sun
contain the light of a prophetic sea.
Suspected, ill at ease, the narrow man
who watches from outside the Paris Bar,
who knows the nomenclature of the saints,
has forsaken all of these and greets
the animals we wear. If he should suddenly
strike out his thundering eyes upon us,
we could be silent, but for how long?
The fountain's children sail their boats

through floods of hunger, and remain
on the streaming stones long after we have danced.
Well, it is still night; the parvenus
sip ice-cold languor, discuss the latest bill.
Like innocence or fever, like the Spring,
a passing madness shuts the music off,
and brings for one heretic moment one white cat
bearing her mark of suffering to these old things.

Ever since Greencastle

Ever since Greencastle
where I boarded the train,
crossing the bed of foamflowers
that slept beside the shed,
I have played a part, I have brazened
it out in the gentian gardens, the cafeteria,
the auditorium, everywhere.
I was none too steady after the fruit punch.
The girl on the coin winked twice
as I dressed for dinner at eight and the reception.
Thank you, thank you all. No applause please.
Having seen you once I didn't dare
to turn my head, those bees swarmed out of your eyes.
I fastened mine on my book
all about the new mathematics.
But you touched me first with a hot bee pressed
to the small of my back, sent my shivers of nerves
humming like quick black birds
in a dangerous sky. Later you said,
"But I saw you at Greencastle. You looked proud."
Proud! I saw us lying together on some enormous shore,
folded like leaves that have spun
down in a draft, lulled by the low sounds of gulls
and our names forgotten.
But you were always so far away.
I turned to discover the slope of your neck
bending toward someone else.
I smiled on my imaginary stage,
performed in the spot of an amber lens.

And you. You were cornered, I presume,
back to the wall and swollen with success.
Barbecued on their hot smiles.
Ah, my well-done turned-to-perfection morsel,
who is the white lamb, who
the ravenous one that blessed the fire?
We lifted a departing toast
to our separate ways, and as if in a dream
I remember our only silence.
How we turned face to face
in the cruelest part of the night.
How we curled to each other
with never a sound to save us.

Elysian Jumps

Dreams of Ships on a Sea at Night

"Where are you going and what do you wish?"
the old moon asked the three.
"We have come to fish for the herring fish
that live in this beautiful sea."
                    —From a nursery rhyme

The stars are coming towards me at a great rate.
Faster and faster, they don't know how to stop.
With a hard stroke of oars, with the sound
of years falling, going to the bottom,
the longboat is off from the breakers.
It has taken so long to find this passage
and now as I stand in the bow the water
hardly reflects me because my edges are melting.
This candle I've been lighting for years
burns a hole in the gauze I've wrapped my life in.
I let it drop into the sea, a dangerous burden.

Now I am equal to this emergency.
I have not resisted the sorrow of emptiness
but have accepted it with both hands
like a true lover. Fish with alarmed eyes
have memorized every hope in this sea.
I shake off their alarms with my bells
and my brilliant stones, one in each knot
of my net. I must be merciless with my hands,
I must be quick with my stories of gates closing,
of cold water that tastes of sulphur and solitude.
I kneel like a bush in my darkness.

❁

Before I learned to fish I was a common sailor
dreaming against the mast with my arms
crossed peacefully. That was my childhood.
The stars were quiet then and I was waiting.
Now there is this work, this cruel progress.
The other ships lost out in the salt beds,
the green trundles prepared in the hold.
There are the bells beating against black waves
and murmuring with the tongues of fish.
The thought of them enters my head like a bright sword.
I have all night to please myself with its fine edge
cutting across the heart of my sickness.
All night long I fish until the catch is in.

Before the Dark

The twilight agitates the birds,
they cross the grey sky fitfully,
ruffling the air, disturbing
my heavy swoon into silence.
They leave no mark, the birds,
only that sense of wild energy,
a throbbing like the strings
of an instrument, the electric harp
in my pulse, the thin wing of desire.

The sudden rush of wings like breath
until there is no more light.
In the dark summer night you flung
yourself up and I heard you cry,
"Ah Love, at last I've taken my life
into my own hands."

It is from that terrible height
we are still trying to ascend.
With our birds' wrists beating the air,
sometimes leaving a touch
on one another, sometimes
no more than a senseless stir
slow motioned as dreams
where we shadow each other
from one darkness down to the next.

I have suffered from these dreams.
I have seen the lost wings fall uselessly—

the pain that has no fruit.
I have your old griefs on my face
and a black cockade in my throat
and I am sick of this butchery
that chops desire into two parts.
The red remains of a bird.

There in your other life
you live in a furnished room
and you walk in the snow
with my letters in your pocket.
Now the night is coming down like ashes.

It is hard to go up with this weight
pressing me apart.
I am separated from myself.
I have the days and the nights
and a red stain on my lips
where I have kissed you, Love,
the bird in my flesh.

The Tapestry Roses of A.D. 1959

one

Nothing will sustain like the willow,
green on the snow, open and anointed
with tears of leaves;
and the one blue cup inside the shade.
Or the orange quilt on the mountain
like another sun.
I'll take my chances here.

Might it not be impossible to last the summer?
The years have yet to dry in our dark months,
a long wait lies like a corpse in our bed.
It is not for this we have climbed the hill—
we are looking for the hostel,
the one with edelweiss in all the windows.
We will not travel the dinky trains,
the stations of our journey are too far apart.
Quick, we must decide; will it be summer soon?

two

Who belongs to me tonight?
The criminal cuffed to his captor
has left the train. He had a tender smile
but so did the policeman.
The bargain is always a bad one.

*

Why have they drawn our eyes two asterisks?
We dared that chance that brought us to a mountain
where the grass leans over,
where the flowered windows open and the clouds fly in,
where purple streams below the trees.
I have your lips' hot stamp upon my shoulder,
the delicate bruise of your mouth and eyelash touch.
Maybe we will survive if you don't tell them
I was there, or the way the sun felt,
or of the white streets that sleep
all the way down to the beach,
or of your hands just out of the ocean
that covered me with salt spray.
Keep me inside, make a circle on the mountain.
I will lie down and be the snow for you.

It might be we can tell them anything we like
but must remember that moon rising
over the fiesta square, and the cool rustle
of paper decorations lighting across the cicadas.
How we turned slowly in a dance of violins,
how those drops of wine that gleamed magenta
in the glass seemed almost of our making.
We only knew summer and the sound of bees,
the hot hours heaped like oranges.

three

I was there too, ornamental, white and gold
décolletage flocked by pearls.
Outside the chariots tipped to the ground.
"You are lucky, you know, to live in this historic house.

See how they've taken you in.
Your husband is very proud of you."
The walls are papered with Renoirs;
here every face congratulates itself.
Leaves spinning in the tea of clairvoyantes
settle quickly in an established pattern.
We skimmed it off the top and left the bitterness.
Meanwhile I take hardly space enough for one
and apologize for taking that,
but a music box that plays in some forgotten corner
of my brain suddenly stops, run down.
We have come to the end of tunes.

It must be we listened too long to those
who never celebrate a victory.
They've changed the games to prescriptions
and made it dangerous to live.
Still I say, sleep my love,
in the white room facing north
where the step of the wind is fierce,
the moon a bandage across your gifted face.
Animals are wild in the woods outside your window.

four

This is a dream I had. We were together
in a dark museum, more like a planetarium.
I thought your hand was mine.

Our living rooms prove nothing.
The sun's coins jangle on the windowpane.
I hear the hawthorn overhead.

(It might be Sunday and some men
have passed this way, coatless.)
Surely it will soon be spring!
I shall tell you I am almost on my way,
tell you I am not so still,
say the wind is strong today,
a horned forked thing of struts and wheelings.
Say somewhere the mistral left a trace
of wings across my eyes.
Say trust me with your memory,
say give me the world again.

What renaissance I've had was born out of the sea
whose Botticelli waves made me
as beautiful as you. We were all familiars then
of grottos long forsaken by the wind,
we adventured in those diamond sands,
caught with our arms outstretched
pressing the sky apart.

five

It is not beyond me to remember where
we took the evening seriously like squirrels.
And if I listen hard enough I find
your midnight is disconsolate like mine.
What is growing where the earth is new?
I know the sweet rain changes, winter comes;
black spires of pain move forward.

Ah, we cannot forget those hard tribunals
of the night who find us wanting.

But I think we can learn the language of the sea,
lie a moment on the sand, and not look back
to see how we are changed.
If you cover me with your arms,
if you liven me with dawns of dandelions and daisies,
kiss me with the slowly turning wheels of morning,
my wonder will be the breeze.
We'll have two cups and a table,
a bed and two chairs.

It is still early! Morning can find us
thousands of miles alone and gone.
Every look isn't a promise—
the nights are cold with wings
that beat against the rain.
No one will save us here.

six

I refuse to forget the houses
painted robin blue and violet
or compromise the sting of a summer night.
The one rose bush on my balcony
pinkens at morning, quickens the afternoon
with rose dust rising like foam on the sea.
Now, after dark, at the performance
(it is the dance of the Zapateados)
she tips her Spanish comb toward me.
Her dress reminds me of my roses, but she is old.
Soon the ways of caution pass too;
she dances now because it is the thing she loves.
Later we say, "Superb. Wasn't it good?"

and crowd a little closer round the table,
smoke to smoke, lean into our lies that seem to save us.
Can we learn not to be undone by caution?
The rose days pass without our notice.

I have been busy looking for the beach on my floor,
then a year is gone, and another.
We know our friends by the way they do their hair.
The lessons become more exacting,
these black-robed streets have forgotten their senses,
that the park is blue in the darkness.
Tonight they are working late in the botanical gardens—
maybe they will open the moongate?
The white trees stretch their feather boughs.
If we meet at the café near the park
we can see the miracles from there.

seven

Why are the years so silent, the devils?
They know every hand might be a weapon.
(obit. Mr. Rappaport, 63; beloved husband
of Rose; manufactured hats for twenty baffling years)
And toward what marriage do we embark?
Now while there still seems to be time
I live like a criminal.
But all the time my heart is trying
to say the beautiful sound of your name.
We speak in undertones but my languor is hot
and red as hibiscus. Will it be later then
that we will sleep to the little sounds
of clocks and clacks of footsteps?

68

Or drink our lemonade on the porch?
The morning glory dots the vine,
sun ladders climb across the blinds.

But miles away I wear green earrings and prepare
an evening at the theatre. Eating grapes
in the balcony I remember my mother.
Oh, be careful of the grass and the creatures
who live between the apple and the leaf!
On the rooftop of my thoughts I move
closer to the edge and call her name.
Her hands tremble on stubs of twigs,
my chances are diminishing.
This morning that came in a haze of refinement
lost me among the teacups and the Aubussons.
Still the birds who remain alive continue singing.
I will always open cages,
even the birds in the tapestries will fly out.

After You've Gone

Somehow I believe the door isn't really closed.
It must be some of your substance sticking
between it and the door frame . . . the rest of you,
an extra hand or eye, some measure,
a low chant or a sigh that wouldn't or couldn't leave
down the long corridor of your footsteps.
And I would give the treasure of my house
if I could shout against this mountain
of a door to call you back. Instead I lean
heavily on myself, a kind of dead tree.

The night will surely pass this way.
I'll settle like dust in a solitary,
extended midnight. For company
I have your voice . . . your lips . . . your mouth.

You left your mouth behind!

An Afternoon Nap

It is a bright afternoon full of sun.
As for me, a few flakes of dust
go down with me as I sink. I go down
as if from a far distance
with my hands feathery.
Quills scribbling on air.

The room is furious with too much sun.
Like a sprinter I come
to the catacombs with a key
still in my hand—to the last
gasp of the string—as if to a special sleep.

Under the lip of a cloud
a bright shape hurries away,
a musical shape, a creature
breathing the light,
that needs only light to breathe.

The dust is heavy on top of me!
O bird without wings.
Bird without a throat, fish
with barnacles for scales.
Quickly, before I forget—
there is a word. The word the pelican sings.
Bird with wings like straps,
chained to the brim of a pool
where the day lies in ruins, where
the tap tap of a drum begins

to drop dark petals. Quickly,
the horizon flickers, its tail unfurls.

I am a wisdom of light!
With a key hot in my hand,
I swear I'll wake soon and work.

In a window across the street
a small hard fist of sun
flashes again, and again.
I take that fist of fire
into my own hands and make it a cry.
One cry, even from this distance,
and I rise like dust, I ascend, I appear.

Bring Me My Blue Rebozo

I don't know what's ahead
I can't tell whether it's a wedding party
we'll be going to later on
or a dangerous journey
I haven't made any reservations anyplace
—but bring me my blue rebozo
because it is woven with rough wild sounds of Mixtec legends
by hands that fashioned the stones in Mitla
before Moctezuma, before Cortes and his party,
before their monumental red and orange gods
were blanched out forever
bring me my blue rebozo
smell of dust and the zocolo in Oaxaca
smell of dust and the market place on Saturday
stray dogs and burros and black angels
smell of green baskets, of trips by foot
down sandy mountain paths
smell of dust and the straight white arm of the sun
hitting the Indian laurel in the middle of the zocolo
bring me my blue rebozo
smell of bread and cheese and melon

Was it really so?
sitting under the laurel the glistening leaves
made a hollow bell a high green cave
and the stillness only muted not broken
by the rolling of marimbas

●

Sharing a bench in the zocolo
with a man whose brown and ardent face
wore a crown of white hair we watched
the children pass and wondered
if they were going home for lunch
and knew it wasn't true

many of them were forbidden to beg
so we ate casually as if sitting there
were an ordinary thing while all the while
the sacrificial city opened its heart
and gave its victims to us to see

Sometimes I seem to know what's ahead
I have caught glimpses of inner fountains
surrounded by high red flowers
and a wall of mountains crowded with former strays
celebrating a university

I have come for you, are you ready?
Sundays are washed by rivers of fiestas
whose names are Consuelo and Turibio, Manuel and Raul.

The Long Way Round to Rome

Leaves of the garden square in Soho are falling;
good green leaves still, September is young in the air.
I sit on a bench near a flowering bush,
pigeons are at my feet—the sound of their wings
flutters over these pages. I have come
down Sunday avenues of reasonable dreams
where distance escapes through the hedges.

Another afternoon when the sun was a hatchet of gold
that struck upon my thighs and shimmered there
I was one small advance away from caution.
Now I'm awakened by furious dreams;
my pastiche spectacles don't comfort me.
Now when they recommend their medicines, like time,
I only hear some shivering among us.
I remember our goodbye.

Do you think they have made me poorer than you?
Have they taken my arms for sticks to flap in the wind?
And yet with you I never slept a concrete sleep
nor learned to exorcise the threadbare faces
and the lost footsteps falling.
They are falling now with the leaves.

A yellow rain was flooding the window
all the way down from Milano.
I saw it could be anywhere. . . .
                    My dead father wears a red carnation
                    which in life he never wore;

at his throat a bunch of yellow grapes
and at his fingers threads of vines.
His name in the waving meadow
is juniper and thyme
and the janitor of dust is sweeping
his fortune into my breath.

Remembering the pattern of the sundown trees
against the plate-glass frontage of Avenue Matignon,
echoing the living leaves,
the boulevards that fall away,
the gramophone playing in the next dark room,
heliotrope and milkweed sing in me
and the fantastic swish of great dresses
rustle in nights I've never known.
The music in my head is more various
than all their restaurants and comedies.
And though formulas I cannot remember
decide my distances, and economies
that are no friends of mine
have limited my procedure,
the last time I drowned I rose lank haired
and managed to breathe again
between the shafts of memory and death.

Soon behind the cloister
of blue fringed window shades
we may stand one periwinkle morning, hand over hand.
I seem to remember a promise
but in fact it is only a cut in the hedge
and the unreasonable sun of a Sunday afternoon
and the wooden beat of wings
and the blush of the last wild heat of summer.

In the half life of that promise
I am quickened again
like all things that dream in amber sunlight
in the silence of leaves and burning greens.

Notes on the Revolution in Cuba

I

There has been talk of a country
which is the footprint made by exotic birds
who danced once, whose calls and colors
still ring like great magenta flowers,
like the sun drenching a curved magenta leaf.
I am not able to tell that fearless color
or even the weight of the night
that falls around your shoulders there.
It should be somewhere between lightness and laughter
and the moon's weight that treads the waters of Havana
embroidered with strings of mandolins.
If it is heavier than these, if it is heavy
with much traffic in the gorgeous currency of love
then beauty has become no more or less than this:
the actual colors of feeling
that all pile up like treasures in a crowded room
where nothing really gets old and nothing
is thrown away. The pattern of beauty
lasts on these feelings
stronger for what I know.

And if I don't know exactly the texture
of the language there, I have been pierced
by its sweetness, by its actual conversations,
by its banners. Remember, *"Si ahora Cuba es feliz."*
What more is there to know of a language
which is old, stricken many times and betrayed?
What more is there to know than the truth

of these banners which sprang in a mountain camp,
whose revolution sped through villages
like incorruptible hope, like the certainty
of knowledge, which decorate the air
as if a tree had shed a million leaves
and woven them through the afternoon
of bus drivers and shoeshine boys.
These waving colors really belong to them,
they are repeated and caught in their greetings.
What words do I know to deny them?
This streaming down the long shadows of the Malecon
is bright as the intimate colors of feeling.

Despite its beauty then I must remember Cuba
because I have a clock that ticks that hour and that place
as if time stopped ecstatically.
Where are the clocks not stopped in high human matters?
Where are the urgent bells not pealing minutely
in the inmost mechanisms?
It is the human heart I'm after.
It is the beauty of cardinal feelings and language
that races through the veins of memory.
It is this I'm after, it is these sentient banners
flocking Cuba releasing their colors
to gladden us to valor.

And the brightest color is the hero.
His life is an intimate part of our day.
His color is justice and the serious struggle
never finished, implicit in his banner.
The brightest color is the hero
yet heroism isn't what he seems to be
in this moment or that one. It isn't

his apostolic head or the legend about him
true as it is. The cardinal heart of his struggle
is necessity. In this he shows us the way to be heroic.
For this we do not praise him, or pray for him:
we thank him, we cherish him. He is our secret color.

II

Let your daughters walk one passage
through the evening and lie in hopeless
ignorance in rooms where tricks of color
register some garble on the window,
where angels crack and tumble from the ceiling.
Let your father bear a number in the spot
he likes to sport a white carnation
or a badge of honor; let him limp, weave
through tattered webs of men to find
the cheapest restaurant (and even there
a multitude of meats and cheese deny
his poverty). Let his hunger choose
and having chosen, eat, standing all the while;
then let him fall back into the night
to sell his numbers. Let your son
leave school, before he learns to read or write
and spend his skinny legs bending
among the heavy stalks of sugar.
Then you will know these desperations
are no disorder of the blood or mind,
merely by hazard of rebirth could be your own.
Then you will find a place among the hills
and grow your hair and beard,
come down to Havana in a storm of men
distinguished from the frauds of government

and the taste in the streaming wind
will be the sweet white grains of liberty.

III

I sleep in the twin earths of a broken street
while time lies along my arm
or at my feet. I lie in a narrow bed
and see the smallest stars are children
who play among the mandolins on tiptoe.
One is a little boy whose brown legs know
a hundred hallways, those legs that wince
and thrust their way beneath a shoeshine box
or lotteries, supple and swift through darkness
have never known the freedom of a fountain
or the legend of a mountain stream.
Tonight I wake to hear the birthday of the year
is shouted in the streets and one bright candle
sings on top the revolution's cake.
Through the clasp of jubilant eyes
the fountains run with exultation.
I cannot deny this prize.
To not deny is almost to achieve.

In the morning the sun will be sweet
on the animal cages where parrots, dogs and kittens
are waiting to be loved enough.
We are all waiting but confused by ancient messages,
"Do not look too far out of your eyes
or seek new colors!"

But even in the step of a limping man
my eyes discern an unprecedented green.

Prophet Says We Live in Hell

The ponderous swimmer
fastened by one cord like a newborn infant
still attached to its mother
makes his first cry, the gurgle
of oxygen bubbles, into the universe.
The white frog that is Leonov,
cumbersome and grainy, rushes forward
through the black and white magic lantern
of an orbit with the sun on one shoulder
and the moon on the other.

But Where There Is Hell

Midnight in New York: 11 PM in Peoria:
6 AM in Florence: 7 AM in Athens:
Leonov is crawling over his spaceship
on the outside, a white fly
with a hammer and a screwdriver,
sees a flaming red band rising
over the earth smashing a path across the black
asphaltum of infinity. While Leonov
cracks the future open like a ripe watermelon
clustered with seeds of stars
a child sleeps lightly in Peoria.

There Must Be Paradise